# *THIS WAY*
## but
# *NOT HERE*

---

## *An Ode to*
## *Lake Champlain*

*Mathias Dubilier*

Burlington, Vermont

Onion River Press
89 Church Street
Burlington, VT 05401
info@onionriverpress.com
www.onionriverpress.com

ISBN: 978-1-966607-41-0

Library of Congress Control Number: 2026905176

# Table of Contents


1   I'm in Love With a Lake.................................... 1

2   Allow Me to Introduce Myself ....................... 8

3   The Oldest Place in the World....................... 17

4   I Haven't Forgotten: The Oldest Place .......... 27

5   OK, But First This One Special Place ............. 32

6   Now for Real: The Oldest Place ...................... 37

7   Odziohozo ...................................................... 42

8   I Was Warned About This Kind of Work........ 48

9   Juniper Island ............................................... 55

10  OK, for Real Now: Juniper Island .................. 66

11  Have You Seen the Lake Monster?................... 81

12  Cliff Jumpers and a Drowning....................... 89

13  Cliff Jumpers: For Real .................................. 95

14  The Sunset: Forgiveness and Promise ............ 106

15  This Way But Not Here .................................. 110

Acknowledgments ........................................... 114

To Kirsten

You Are My This Way

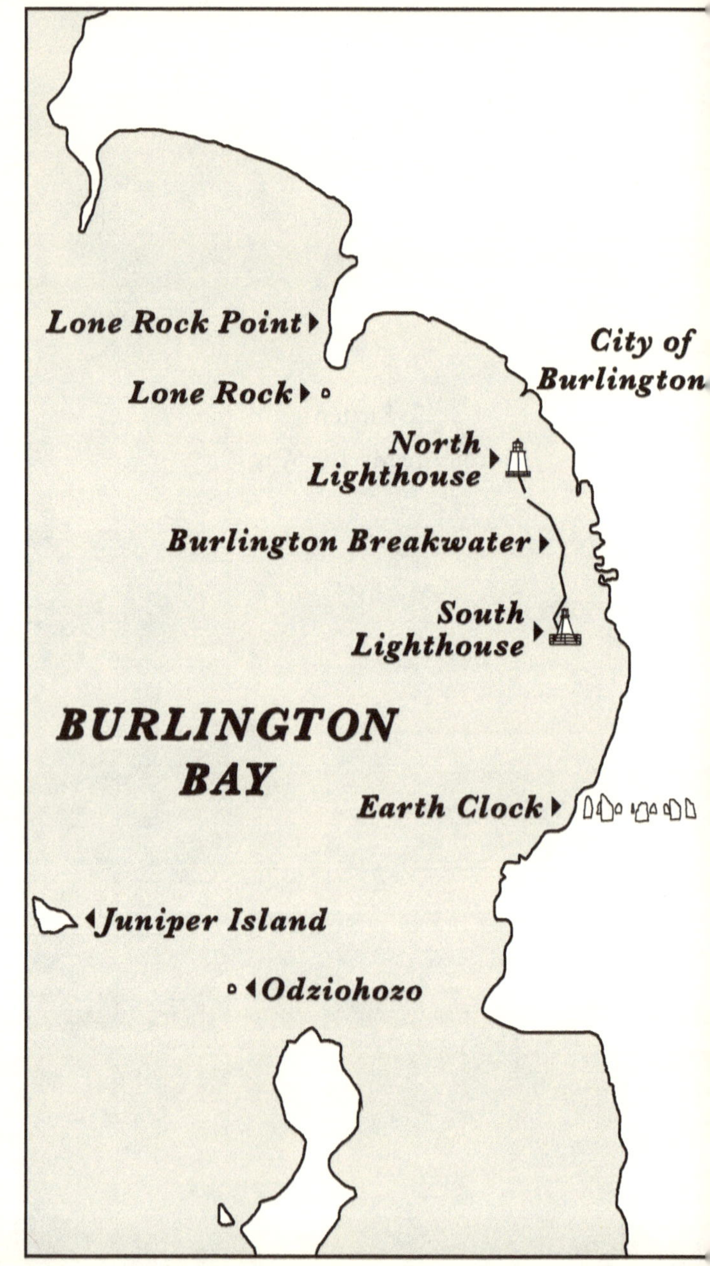

Lone Rock Point ▶
Lone Rock ▶ ○
City of Burlington
North Lighthouse ▶
Burlington Breakwater ▶
South Lighthouse ▶
BURLINGTON BAY
Earth Clock ▶
○ ◀ Juniper Island
○ ◀ Odziohozo

# 1

# *I'm in Love With a Lake*

I'm in love with a lake.

I say that so plainly as if I knew what I was saying, but the truth is, I don't. I first met Lake Champlain almost 50 years ago, and I have been living near her ever since. But even after all those decades, I still don't fully understand the lake or my attraction to her. What is my connection? Can I call this a love affair?

Is it possible to talk about love for an inanimate object?

But then again, to me, the lake is not an inanimate object. She is alive. She is an ancient being.

Lake Champlain is one of the United States' larger lakes. She straddles the border with Canada, between Vermont and New York, and has a history of biology, geology, geopolitical battles, and lore that makes her absolutely unique. She is largely undeveloped, and so you can be on Lake Champlain and experience what the world looked like long before any humans arrived here. The more time I spend on Lake Champlain, and the better I get to know her, the more I feel that I am connecting with something deeper. Lake Champlain is nature's daughter, and to me she is beautiful and alluring and she commands my respect.

In the last 10 years, I have deepened my relationship with Lake Champlain by becoming a tour boat captain. I take people out on a small boat and tell stories. Some of the stories are about the lake's history, some about her lore, and some about her place in my heart. It's that last category that keeps changing. Well, actually, they all keep changing because I keep on learning more about Lake Champlain. To me, she is endlessly fascinating.

Welcome aboard. My name is Mathias.

Just as I introduce myself to my guests aboard my tour boat and provide a little preview of what they will be experiencing during the two-hour cruise out on Lake Champlain, I'll tell you what you can expect from our time together.

Lies. That's what you'll hear. I always warn

everyone right away. I don't know all the facts, but I'll tell you a story.

That's partly because some of even the most basic facts are squishy. Her length, for instance. She is, as she lies in the valley between the Green Mountains and the Adirondacks, about 115 miles long.

I'm always using "about" or "-ish," or I throw in an "or so." Sometimes I will tell you outright: I'm a terrible tour guide. All summer long, I tell these little lies to entertain you, and all winter long I research the truth so I can close the gap between truths and lies for next summer's guests.

That line always gets a laugh.

It might be funny, but it hides a truth: As odd as it may sound about something as old and evidentiary as the lake, there is no firm agreement on some of her most basic facts. Sometimes I'm just honest and tell you the lake is somewhere between 100 and just over 120 miles long, depending on whom you ask and what standards you use to define what constitutes a lake.

To me, her southern end is a river, not a lake. I love that Lake Champlain transforms from river to lake and back to river again on her northern end. We all have different parts of our personality that transmute. We are childish in some ways, mature in others. Am I really 64 years old? Part of me is certainly not. The older I get and the more confident I become, the more I allow myself to become childish again.

Or, for instance: I am the consummate extrovert while narrating boat tours. I love being the outgoing, confidently conversational, and sometimes almost brazen Capt. Matty Black. At home, I have a deep-seated need to hole up in my quarters and avoid as much human contact as I can justify, while still appearing to be polite and reasonably part of the various communities to which I belong.

Some of the approximations I offer about the lake are not due to my laziness in research or lack of ability to memorize material, but to an evolution of technology. Regarding her depth, for example.

When I had my first sailboat with a keel in the 1980s, my depth sounder was of a vintage that didn't probe deeper than 200 feet. The charts at the time showed the lake's deepest spots to be in the 300-foot range. My sailboat now has a sonar that goes to 400 feet. More expensive equipment on science boats includes side scan sonar that provides more dimensional imaging, and today remotely operated vehicles are available as well. These days, the lake's deepest spot is reported to be somewhere between 400 and 433 feet, depending on the source.

What does it mean to love someone? Am I less of a committed partner to my wife because I don't know the amount of blood coursing through her veins or the pulsing sequence of ventricles in her heart? Must I know Lake Champlain's bathymetry to love her? How many species of her fish must I know? Some, surely. Her endangered sturgeon, for one, because it might be what some say is the mythical sea creature Champ.

But also her landlocked salmon. To love Lake Champlain is to understand how the Atlantic fish came to make its home in the lake's fresh water.

What a story! Talk about transformation! The story is about how, sometime after Pangea and at the end of the ice age, as the glaciers melted, they left this area depressed so far below sea level that the newly formed Atlantic Ocean rushed in and created the Champlain Sea.

In which all manner of sea creatures lived. Including at least one that became Champ, the sea serpent of Lake Champlain.

How much of her geological history must I know? How much about the humans who first came to live on her shores as the glaciers receded? On tours, sometimes people ask me how many miles of shoreline there are. How much water is in the lake?

I laugh and shrug and admit that I am a horrible tour guide and don't know.

I don't relate to Lake Champlain through these statistics. But I don't say that.

Even though I feel my answer makes me seem like an uninformed tour guide, it's the honest answer. Maybe I smirk and shrug as a way of hiding what I really feel. Maybe being cavalier allows me to keep the essence of my love for Lake Champlain a secret.

It's not about the numbers. Go ahead: Think I'm not that invested.

I look out over the water of so many moods. For a moment, just by having something to hide, I am OK with not knowing what lies at the bottom of my feelings for this mysterious and immense being called Lake Champlain.

My love for the lake is something more inexplicable. It's both maternal and partakes of the same feelings I have for my wife. Attraction. A bit of mystery. Allure. Respect. Admiration. Profound gratitude. There is no scale to these feelings. No quantification. They swirl. They eddy. They flood and ebb.

Even when I am elsewhere, and land based, all I have to do is imagine the broad lake bulging into Burlington Bay and lapping against the sandy shore, and my entire being fills with a sense of ease. The lake absorbs.

Unload, she says to me. Unbear yourself. Let go. Give it all to me if you need a place for it.

Lake Champlain absorbs without judgement. Unconditionally.

I feel better just living close to her shores. When I am driving or walking and catch a glimpse of her, I breathe easier. Deeper. Living close to Lake Champlain helps me live a healthier life. She is my doctor and my guru. She is my shaman and my genie. Goddess and lover.

# 2

# *Allow Me To Introduce Myself*

This profession of introducing people to Lake Champlain gives me so much pleasure but causes me so much confusion, because I am constantly asking myself if I am selling out what I profess to love so dearly: Lake Champlain.

Is tourism inherently a bad thing, or are there benefits?

For me, the benefits would have to go beyond the sales tax I generate for the City of Burlington and the State of Vermont.

Does tourism always exploit? Or can it be sustainable? Could it possibly even be beneficial?

The thing is, I've been to tourist towns on the off season. It's scary to see only vestiges of life in them. It's like seeing the empty fare rides after everyone has gone home. Some say the locals can finally spread their elbows, but I'm a cynic. I see two groups at the watering holes on Commercial Street in Provincetown after Labor Day. Those who don't know how it used to be when the town made its living off the sea, and the few who still do, but won't be around to raise another generation.

Tourism saps the local blood from a place. Jobs are seasonal, rents unaffordable.

I love Burlington. I don't want it to become a Provincetown. What am I doing in the tourism business?

Being a tour guide of an entity that perplexes me and still eludes me in many ways intensifies my conflict. There's a hidden shame every time I utter a date and know that it might be off. Every time I cobble together a few facts about the indigenous people, but I can't recall all the details from the material I have read. Every time I'm asked about which pollutant contributes most to the lake.

I was born into a water family in New York City. When I was a kid, my family vacationed in Fire Island Pines in houses near the beach or on the bay side. As teenagers, my dad took us bluefishing in his 21-foot center console in Long Island Sound. For a couple weeks every summer, he would rent a ramshackle little cabin on a lake up in Quebec and that's where I learned how to row a dinghy and sail a homemade Sunfish type of rig.

When my parents divorced and my German mother took us four kids back to her homeland, I lived in Germany from 10 to 18. We would spend some vacations on my uncle's sailboat on Lake Constance. He had a large wooden sailboat, and I remember the evening when I was in the V-berth, and my cousin showed me how to climb out of the forward hatch, and we lay on the deck looking at the stars, and I thought there was nothing more romantic in the world than owning a sailboat.

In my late teens, when I moved to Burlington to live with my dad again, I had a windsurfer. In my twenties, I bought a Lightning, a small wooden sailboat with a retractable centerboard. In my thirties I bought a 25-foot Cape Dory sailboat with a fixed keel. And in my forties I bought a 33-foot Hans Christian, an ocean-faring sailboat. In my fifties, I set out on that boat from Lake Champlain, down the Hudson River, across the Atlantic, and crisscross throughout the

Mediterranean. It was a three-year voyage until I was back in my home waters of Lake Champlain.

Before returning, I already knew what I wanted to do once I was home: First, I was looking forward to falling in love again with my home waters and getting to know the lake even better. And the other thing I knew I would do was get into the tour boat business so I could share my love of the lake with others. I couldn't imagine a better job.

I was the quintessential Odysseus who was coming home to Ithaca, and I wanted to share my love of home with everyone who would listen.

I bought an existing tour operation with a traditional sailboat. It was a Friendship sloop with wooden spars and traditional rigging. It could handle up to a dozen passengers in its large cockpit.

As a sailor, I was excited to finally own a traditional gaff rig. But as a tour guide, I had a problem. It had been some 40 years since I first moved to Burlington and fell in love with Lake Champlain, and while I loved the lake and had sailed on her for decades, I still didn't know many facts about her. I started to read books and research online websites. I had heard some of the lake's stories over the years, but did I know them well enough to be an authoritative tour guide?

I had learned a few of Vermont's iconic stories because during college I had a job driving a small tour bus, picking up guests from a downtown hotel, and giving them an hourlong tour through Chittenden County while telling tales of Vermont's early days. I told the stories of how it came to be that Vermont was developed last among the first colonies and how confusion over who supposedly owned it led to Vermont declaring independence both from Britain and from the other states. Vermont became its own country.

Our country's first civil war was fought between Vermont and the other colonies, I say. It's not an outright lie, but it's an exaggeration because the conflict was before the U.S. was officially a country, so we couldn't technically have a civil war.

They were fun stories to tell because Vermont's independence as a republic is a quintessential American story. A story of mainly of one person, Ethan Allen, standing up against the establishment.

In my early years as a tour boat captain, I leaned heavily on those early republic stories.

But right from the start, I felt they were just the filler to something more important that I wanted to convey: my love for the lake.

She is, with her mostly undeveloped shorelines, dozens of islands, diversity of proportions, quiet coves, foggy mornings, ferocious fall waves, and peaceful homes for fish and fowl, quite simply the most beautiful body of water I have ever seen among all those I have visited throughout Europe, all over the Mediterranean, and in the United States. With her fresh water, she is more pleasant to swim in, and with her numerous natural beaches, she awakens an instinctual yearning to connect with nature, to camp, to sleep near lapping water under a starlit heaven.

But my romantic notions of camping on a beach aren't what you buy a ticket for on my boat. You want the lake's story. So I began to research, and what I found was rather mundane and a story shared by most bodies of water. The shipping industry dominated the lake with the arrival of European settlers, leading to Burlington's explosive growth. The harbor was developed and lighthouses were built. The arrival of the railroad changed everything, as it had everywhere. Before the settlers, indigenous people lived here. Fought with their neighbors. Traded with others. And before that was the ice age, and before that, millions of years of evolution.

All that is nothing that explains my intense feelings of connection with a body of water by which I feel I have been adopted.

I sold the sailing business after a few years. I wanted to spend more time writing. But after a few years, I noticed how much I missed the business of introducing people to my love. Of telling stories that were true-ish, but were really more entertaining than factual.

To get back into the tour business, I bought a motorboat designed exactly for this kind of use. It has a canopy overhead and all the seating is in a circle around a table. It is reminiscent of the first small passenger boats on the lake in the 1800s, which were built with small steam engines.

For an entire summer, my friend and I worked on improving the looks and functions of the boat. We built a fold-out wooden table for picnics. We installed a wooden mast from Holland with bronze navigation lights from Italy. We built a wooden grate for the floor, custom fitting each board to the boat's contours.

And all the while, I asked myself: What exactly

was it that was driving me back into this business? Why did I feel that, more than anything else, I wanted to earn my living by giving people tours on Lake Champlain?

When not working on the boat, I spent time in history books researching the lake's geology, indigenous history, and sea battles during the Revolutionary War.

Before we began working on the boat, I was afraid the boat was too plain to compete in the tour boat business against the romantic wooden-sparred sailboats, and so I told my wife that I needed a name that would put a smile on people's faces as soon as they heard it, even before they saw an image of the boat. Without missing a beat, she answered: *Buttercup.*

Today, I won't be able to be on the lake with you in *Buttercup* and feel the breezes or hear the water lapping against the hull. All we will have are my words. I hope they are sufficient consolation. Here are some of the things I will be sharing with you:

- You will find out why this is the oldest place in the world.

- You will learn about the only island inside the continental U.S. that is a separate country.
- Did you know that Lake Champlain has a sea monster that once was so famous that Scotland got jealous and invented a copycat called the Loch Ness Monster?
- And maybe, if we're lucky, you'll get to see some suicidal maniacs jumping off a cliff.

I'm sorry we're not on the lake right now, but I hope that if you stick with me, you'll get a sense of something deeper I'm trying to get at that I can't during my actual excursions.

# 3

# *The Oldest Place in the World*

All tour guides want to have a superlative in their offerings. The oldest. The biggest. The smallest. The most something.

It's a cheap thrill to satisfy that human desire to get something special and unique. Only here. Only on this tour. Only you get to see this, experience this, witness this. Step right up. Right this way.

At the end of the day, and at the beginning of every cruise, I am also just a tour guide and I fall into the habit of hawking cheap thrills.

At the beginning of the tour, while you and the other guests are still settling into your seats, I tell you that today, when we head out into Lake Champlain, we will be heading out into the oldest part of the world.

As with every group, one or two heads will do that silent half turn in my direction, as if to say, "Did I just hear that right?"

Oldest place in the world? In small, little Vermont? How can that be? I egg on your disbelief as part of my schtick. I vocalize your incredulity outright: "That's got to be some exaggeration that I am making up just because that's what tour guides do, right? We always have to tout that we have the oldest or biggest something."

I fire up the 30-horsepower diesel engine and step onto the dock to slip the lines. I sling back onto the boat and, from the helm, I maneuver out into the harbor.

Before we get to the oldest part of the world, I want to show you one of the reasons I fell in love with Burlington. As we pull out into the harbor, we can begin to see the waterfront as a whole.

It is one gigantic park. Greens that host festivals in summer. A boardwalk along the water's edge with swings for lovers, families, and the lone book reader. Bikers snake through the downtown part of a recreation path that hugs the shoreline all the way up to the next town and then out onto the water on an old railroad causeway.

There's an ice cream stand. There's a

youth-oriented science and nature museum. There is the community-owned boathouse that you walked through to get to my boat slip among all the other boats docked here for the season or used by the hour, as people from all over the lake motor over and park here as easily as you would your car before eating in one of the many lakeside restaurants.

Later, when we are just a bit farther out, you will see our small town is set on a hill overlooking the bay. Typical New England town: red brick churches and two-story painted clapboard houses. Whole patches of the city will be blooming with tree canopies. You will see Burlington, hugged by woods to the north and south.

I had never seen anything like it, having grown up in New York City and Wiesbaden. I remember the first time I saw Burlington like this, but I'll get to that story later.

For now, let me point out the steeples of Burlington.

There are seven we can see from the water. Starting out, on the skyline to the left, north, is the golden-domed Ira Allen Chapel and two fingers to the right, or south, is Old Mill, the first building of the University of Vermont when it was founded in 1801.

I hold my hand straight out and with two fingers against the horizon. This is how we measure distances on the water. You'll see me doing that on this little voyage of ours.

The red spire of Old Mill is two fingers south of Ira Allen Chapel.

By the way, it's a lie that it was UVM's first building. The first one burned in 1824 and was replaced with the one you're looking at. But firsts are always like my grandfather's axe. I've replaced the handle three times and the axe-head once, but it's still my grandfather's axe.

Down in the city, we see City Hall's tower, First Baptist Church, First Congregational Church, First Universal Unitarian Church, and all the way to the right, St. Joseph's, the pride of the once predominantly Catholic Old North End.

The trees in the forefront on Battery Street are hiding the tower of the Cathedral Church of St. Paul, that concrete Brutalist church dumped on Burlington after city planners (in a fervor that swept through so many cities) demolished the German and Italian neighborhoods in the name of urban renewal.

My poetry teacher at UVM was Robert W. Caswell, whose poetry in his book *The Compass of the Heart* is about growing up in the Italian neighborhood of Burlington. A little bit of me fell more deeply in love with Burlington when I read his book, which still stands today on a shelf in my poetry collection in my quarters at home.

What we see from the water is Burlington in layers: starting from the late 1900s close to the water, a hundred years back in the next layer, and up on the skyline, closer to 200 years.

Having grown up in Europe, I look at Burlington and think: So young a city! In so young a country.

Who will we be in a fraction of the time that has passed since this place was last formed by nature?

Behind Burlington's skyline, once we are out far enough, you will see the spine of the Green Mountains.

My town's skyline against my home's mountains: That is my view while at work almost every day out on the lake in summer. I have the best job in the world.

Right now, here we are, in front of the Burlington Community Boathouse. The boathouse is the center of a community-owned marina with slips for the season and some by the hour, so boaters can dock and get lunch at the restaurant with umbrella-covered tables on the dock outside the boathouse. It's always fullest around sunset.

I find this every bit as romantic as any of the ports I sailed into on the Mediterranean.

When I moved here in 1978, the entire waterfront was an industrial wasteland. Most of the land was covered in rail lines and littered with garbage. Huge fuel tanks towered right on the water's edge. There were warehouses, grain towers, a junkyard, a defunct coal-burning electrical plant, and abandoned railcars in which the homeless camped.

It was such an ugly and inaccessible tract of land that 10 years earlier, during urban renewal, the general idea was that it was best suited for a spur of the highway to bring people right into downtown Burlington.

Then, in 1982, when I was 22, Bernie Sanders was elected mayor. Besides another in California, he was the only socialist mayor in the United States. I had just returned from living in socialist Germany. To me there was something comforting about someone proudly believing in government and that it should be funded by those who had money to help those in greater need.

It was thrilling to watch Bernie work toward a goal of converting the waterfront from corporate ownership of contaminating operations to public parklands providing community access to the lake. It made me proud to live here. I like living in a city that consistently votes to spend money on greater harmony between infrastructure and nature.

If we can do it here, then maybe there is hope for humanity.

We'll get to the oldest place in the world soon, but first I pull into a channel between two marinas and take us closer to shore again to look at a prominence next to a building that housed Vermont's navy reserve from 1948 to 1995.

I like visiting this spot because standing here now on this little spit of land is a statue, commissioned by the U.S. Navy, called *The Lone Sailor*.

The original bronze statue was forged in 1987 with artifacts from eight navy ships, and it stands on the Navy Memorial Plaza in Washington, D.C. It honors all who serve and have served in the United States sea services.

In 2018, Burlington was awarded the seventh

copy of that statue, and it was the first to stand on civilian ground.

I am a civilian, but my work as captain falls under the category of merchant marine, and so *The Lone Sailor* was meant to honor me as well. *The Lone Sailor* reminds me to take my work seriously and that even the merchant services have their place and responsibilities.

Just a bit larger than life-size, the sailor is simply standing. At rest for a moment. His duffel stands within arm's reach. He looks out over the water. We can tell it's a blustery day because his pants are ceased against his legs. His peacoat is buttoned and his hands are sheltered in the pockets. He looks west. Toward the sunset.

The statue is surrounded by granite blocks with bronze plaques detailing two historic naval conflicts fought on Lake Champlain, along with words to honor U.S. mariners.

When I visit the memorial on land, my eyes seek out my favorite line engraved into one of the bronze plaques:

"The sailor never fully leaves the sea."

I know everyone projects something different into the mind of The Lone Sailor: maybe adventure or resolve. Or maybe sorrow or missing home.

To me, The Lone Sailor gives me permission to be at rest, to finally settle into a permanent home, while reassuring me: All my memories will forever keep me returning to the sea, and I will always remember everything the sea has taught me.

The Lone Sailor guards the harbor of my Ithaca. I have returned, and part of me has never left my voyage. I fight life's headwinds. I deal with gales that throw me off course. I appreciate every sunset I have the good fortune of seeing.

After leaving The Lone Sailor, we head south through the harbor inside the calm waters sheltered by the breakwater, which was built in the mid-1800s and rebuilt several times. The first time, by constructing wooden cribs on the ice, filling them with stones, and then sinking them to create the foundation of the protective wall for a harbor that was exploding with commerce after Lake Champlain had been connected with the Hudson River by canal in the 1820s.

Beyond the breakwater, the water becomes just a bit rougher, but today it's not amounting to more than just a ripple on the water.

You can see when little gusts of wind brush down onto the surface and whisk along in cat-tails of sharper tiny wavelets and darker water. In sailing school, you're taught to count down until the gust hits the boat and that's exactly when you tack.

*4*

# *I Haven't Forgotten:*
# *The Oldest Place*

Something happens to us when we venture out onto water. We experience a profound shift in how we perceive. Because of that shift, we react differently to our surroundings. We become a different type of animal when we are out on water. More ancient parts of our bodies are woken. Deeper desires stir. We feel more connected to the foundational truths of our beings.

Even when we are not aware of these changes within ourselves, they are happening. It is like atmospheric pressure. It affects us in ways we aren't necessarily aware of or can't describe in so many words. We just feel different.

Most people don't know this. But they know *about* this, and that is why they seek out a tour on a boat in the first place. They could pick out any number of land-based activities, but they chose a boat tour. They are drawn to water.

They feel the water will absorb something that needs to get out. Some excess in their body. It can feel like an energy that needs to be drained. It can feel like a too-busy mind. Water provides a surrounding that allows us to feel in a way we otherwise can't.

I remember one particular day in my late teens. It was summer. I was still settling into my new life in Burlington. I took my windsurfer down to what today is called Blanchard Beach and is part of Oakledge Park. I rigged the sail in the sand and then assembled sail and board in knee-deep water. I got up, caught the wind, and headed out in a fantastic breeze, straight for the Adirondacks on the opposite side of the lake. I had gone about a mile or so when I dipped my sail and turned around to head back. As soon as I turned, I looked back and saw the city of Burlington crouched on the shore of Lake Champlain.

I had never seen the city as a whole. And now, there it was: Burlington. From the Old North End to the university buildings on the skyline to the wooded South End and Hill Section. Burlington. My new home.

Something deep inside clenched hard at this vision. I felt so many emotions at once: I was impressed by the beauty of this small town along the shoreline. I was so grateful that I got to call this place home. I remember those phrases looping repeatedly through my mind: There is Burlington. This is my home.

The only other way to see land from a different perspective is from a plane, but then we are so high and looking down. Water gives us the only chance to get away and look back and see where we have come from, where we live.

When we see land from a different perspective, it inevitably makes us see life from a different perspective.

I had known Burlington. I had walked its streets. I had biked all over the university. I knew the shortcuts through the Hill Section. But seeing Burlington from the lake made me suddenly see the city as a whole. Only by being out on the water and looking back could I recognize what should have been obvious to me after moving to Burlington to live with my father: Burlington, this city by the lake, was my home.

Burlington, Vermont, and Lake Champlain are enmeshed within me. All three. Sometimes they are all one, exuding one blended sense of home and homeland. And often I feel they combine into one maternal being that has adopted me. I feel protected living here. I feel safe. I feel like I belong.

I want to tell you stories about why that is and how that came to be, and my hope is that it will foster your relationship with Lake Champlain, or perhaps it will make you realize that all along, you have had feelings for your own particular home waters or place where you live.

Many of the world's ills stem from us having become too detached from place. We have lost our relationship to where we live.

My neighbor says he is considering a move to Florida because of taxes. What kind of life are we living if it's in relationship to taxes instead of place?

On the other side of the spectrum is a person I heard on the radio who felt restless and homeless in Manhattan until she became a tour guide and learned the history of the place. How inspiring to hear from somebody who found home even amid the honking bustle and pickpocketing thievery of a city like New York.

We fear the conversation about place because

we dread the consequences arising from responsibility to place.

Snow birds have northern and southern addresses for convenience and so are not fully beholden to either. They migrate, but they have no home. Home is the beating heart of place.

**5**

# *OK, But First This One Special Place*

I have not forgotten my promise to tell you about the oldest place in the world. But now we have arrived at Oakledge Park, and I want to show you something else first.

I call it Burlington's mini Stonehenge, but officially it's Burlington's Earth Clock. There are 14 rough-shaped blocks of granite in a circle around an array on the ground that works like a sundial. If you stand in the middle of the circle on a sunny day, your shadow will reveal what time it is.

That gets an "Oh, cool" from you and the other guests. Then I turn toward the Adirondacks and wave my arm across that vista and keep talking. "As a mini Stonehenge, it is built to take advantage of this natural sundial."

On the longest day of the year, the summer

solstice, "the sun sets just about there"—I point northwest toward where the Adirondack Mountains begin to flatten out. "And if you stand in the middle of the Earth Clock, one of the granite stones will be aligned exactly with where the sun sets on that day."

And then, all summer long, the sun sets farther and farther south, I say as my outstretched hand bounces along the horizon, "and today, for instance, the sun will set just about there." My arm is now pointing to a spot on the skyline farther south but just north of Juniper Island. "And if you stand in the middle of the Earth Clock on December 21 or the shortest day of the year, one of the stones will align with where the sun will set—just about there, south of Juniper Island."

What follows is stillness from all of you. You all gaze out over the mountainous skyline to the west. There's no photo to take with your devices because it's not sunset yet. All there is is your imagination, now soaring off into alignments and scales of immensity reduced down to earthly measures. This awakens admiration for the most basic of calculations, based on observations that humans have been charting since we first were able to draw a line in dirt with a stick.

This observation and charting is what makes us humans unique among the Earth's animals. I believe this creation of an annual calendar, using the sun and stones, was among the first science practiced by humans.

I let the quiet moment last. I don't say any of what I have just said. I don't think I need to. Let everyone experience it in their own way. Let each of you come to your own conclusions about who we are and what our needs are.

I don't tell you that I relate to that early human because I, too, chart the sun at home. I have a tiny mirror on my southwest-facing windowsill. As the sun appears to sail across the sky, a single ray reflects in that mirror, which glances upward toward the ceiling in my quarters. On certain days, I use a pencil to trace the trajectory of the sun's path across the ceiling.

When I am sitting at my desk in winter and writing, like I am doing right now, I can look up at my ceiling and see—not the Adirondacks—but a bright sun spot among lines that indicate where I am in this trip around the sun: how close to the apogee, which is the solstice; or to an equinox; or to a cross-quarter. In the depths of winter, with the sun so low in the southwestern sky, the line across my ceiling is at its deepest in my quarters.

I don't tell you (because part of me is an introvert) that I consider the work of creating this solar array on my ceiling sacred work. And that it helps me structure my life and keep me in balance between my extroverted summer job as a tour boat captain and my winter life of researching, writing, meditating, and creating sacred practices.

I look up at my ceiling and feel the urgency of the season and how few writing days are left this winter. Or I feel pride at how much I have accomplished. Or I see that in a few days, it will be time again to retreat into absolute solitude, light the candles, and engage in the rituals I continue to refine.

I don't tell you any of this as we begin to motor away from the Earth Clock toward the Adirondacks, because this is your own time to have a conversation with the lake. In a language that isn't spoken.

While researching the Earth Clock, I came across the website of the founder, Ivan McBeth. I wanted to have a conversation with him, and was saddened to see that he had already passed on almost 10 years earlier. But his extensive website is still available.

From that website, I gleamed this excerpt: "I want to make a difference in humanity's—and ultimately this wonderful world's—evolution. I would like to share the many secrets and tools I have either been shown by my teachers, or have discovered and developed myself, in order that people may transform themselves into free souls, and become empowered Caretakers of the Earth."

# 6

# *Now for Real:
The Oldest Place*

I break the quiet with an acknowledgment that it's time to make good on my promise about the oldest place in the world.

As we head out into the lake, I can now turn back toward Vermont and look at the mountainous skyline to the east: the Green Mountains.

I point out Mount Mansfield, which is our highest mountain at 4,200 feet, and I mutter the last part: "something, something." The mutter gets a chuckle because by now you are used to me feeling uncomfortable with always lying, but in this case, the "something, something" is not just a symptom of not remembering or evolving technology, but of the ever-undulating Earth itself. Mount Mansfield used to be listed as one particular height when it was triangulated by sextants back in the day, and then was revised when GPS came along, and then revised again when GPS became more accurate. But here's what we also know: The Green Mountains are eroding. They used to be as high as the Rocky Mountains and they have been eroding ever since.

Moving my finger south along the skyline, I identify Bolton and Camel's Hump, and in a bit, we will see the three-summit ridge of Mount Ellen, Mount Abe, and Mount Lincoln.

Here's the thing, I say. Those are the oldest mountains in the world.

I know, right? The oldest should be somewhere in Asia or Africa, not here, in the New World of the Americas.

Immediately, I start backpedaling. It's another lie, I say. The Green Mountains are part of the Appalachian Mountains, so it's not just "here" that is the oldest part of the world. It's the whole East Coast mountain range of the Appalachians that's the oldest mountain range in the world. Furthermore, Wikipedia has ruined things for tour guides because, while the Appalachians used to be considered the oldest, Wikipedia now parses that into something possibly still plausible, but certainly less definitive.

Like I said, I remind everyone, don't trust me. Lies, all summer long.

But the truth is, I immediately contradict myself, that we are indeed in *an* oldest part of the world. We didn't know it when we started finding odd formations in the rock in a limestone quarry in Isle La Motte in the mid-1800s. Naturalists knew right away that they were fossils of coral reef, but what they didn't know was exactly how old they were. With today's technology, we now know that in a vein under Lake Champlain and Burlington lies the Chazy Reef, the oldest coral reef that we know of in the world.

If I have a local resident aboard, I ask them if they know the mascot of Burlington High School. They do. It's the Seahorses. And yes, they are just as baffled about why as I was when I was a senior at BHS.

Turns out that when workers were digging the foundation of the then high school in the 1920s, the building that is today's middle school on Main Street, they dug up a beautiful seahorse fossil. In honor of our geological heritage, they named the school mascot after that seahorse.

So, in some arguably demonstrable ways, we are in an oldest part of the world. I get to be the tour guide who makes good on an outlandish claim.

Of course, the world didn't always look like it does today. As Heraclitus said, thousands of years before I started giving tours, you can't step into the same river twice. So this part of the world wasn't really this part of the world when the seahorses were swimming here. With plate tectonics, this part of the world was much farther south, and the Atlantic wasn't what it is today. So some might argue, and some on my cruises do, that THIS isn't the oldest part of the world, since it was a different world back then.

To which I freely admit: lies. All summer long, lies, just to keep you entertained.

But others are quiet. Particularly when I have locals aboard, they get quiet. They are feeling that feeling of "that explains it." Long before I became a tour guide, I knew the feeling myself: I would be coming back from a visit out of state, and as soon as I drove across the state line, I inhaled deeper. The mountains may be of the same range, but they have a different feeling here in Vermont.

I used to think it was just me who convinced myself that there was such a sharply different feeling on one side of the White River from the other, but over the years, I have spoken to so many fellow Vermonters who are surprised to find they have that exact same feeling when driving home and crossing the bridge.

I say "that explains it," but nothing is explained by the existence of the Chazy Reef, the oldest coral reef in the world, running under the Champlain Valley. It just leads to more questions. Why here? How and why did life form its first maritime colony in this particular place? What energies were conducive to life on this particular plate? What if the entire basin of Lake Champlain is a type of ley line, or an area that is akin to a chakra within the human body? What if a confluence of certain frequencies meets in this valley, and they are absorbed by this body of water in such a way that they are amplified and can be felt if we allow ourselves to? What might the Earth be trying to telegraph to us? Or is Earth itself just another instrument of something even greater and older, expressing itself in a language it hopes we will try to understand?

When I am sailing on Lake Champlain, it is like being lulled by a foreign tongue. I don't recognize words, but I trust the tone that soothes me.

# 7

# *Odziohozo*

If there is only one story I could tell about Lake Champlain, then it wouldn't be about its mythical sea monster called Champ. It wouldn't be about the sea battles led by Ethan Allen and Benedict Arnold in what some claim to be the Americans' first sea warfare against the British. If I could tell only one story, then I would tell the story of Odziohozo.

I repeat each syllable slowly and clearly. Od – zo – ho – zo. And then I add: "If you can slip an 'i' into that second syllable, then we're getting closer to saying Odziohozo." But, I add, I am a white dude from the 21st century, and I know that an indigenous person from a thousand years ago would be horrified at how I am butchering the pronunciation.

It always gets a chuckle, but it touches on something I want to be cautious about. In the United States, we have undergone a tremendous and long-overdue growth spurt in the last couple of decades, and we have become more sensitive to practices we now recognize as cultural appropriation.

Different sources write his name differently. Today's Wikipedia writes Odziozo, but then specifies an "h" in the pronunciation in the body of the entry. I spell it the way I first saw it in writing so many decades ago I can't remember the source, but I remember wrapping my tongue around the "zio" to make it two syllables.

I am aware that I, as a white person in the 21st century, am telling a story originally told by people who lived here for thousands of years before colonists appeared. Their story was most likely quite different from the one I'll be telling today. But I tell the story because it has grown to mean a lot to me. Odziohozo is a sacred place for the Abenaki. It has become sacred for me as well.

Odziohozo is that rock, right there between Juniper Island and Shelburne Point. To the indigenous people, it is a sacred incarnation of a being that shaped this part of the world and created Lake Champlain.

The story of Odziohozo is the type of story studied today by those in the fields of landscape mythology and geomythology and has roots going back to the Greek concept of euhemerism, which explores the connections between myths and historical events.

As with all oral tradition, there are different versions of the story, and the one that I heard starts before any of the Champlain Valley looked as it does today. The story starts before there were mountains and before there was the lake. There was a being in the earth that was Odziohozo, and he was waking up, or coming into consciousness, if you will, and in doing so, he rolled over to one side and pushed up the Green Mountains, and then he rolled himself over in the other direction and pushed up the Adirondacks. And then Odziohozo clawed himself out of the ground, and in doing so, he created this deep crevasse into which water rushed and formed the lake.

And then Odziohozo towered over this part of the world he had created and was so in love with what he had created that he transformed himself into a pillar of rock in the middle of the lake so that he could forever enjoy the lake.

And, though I didn't hear it this way, I used to add the line "so that he could forever keep watch over the lake and make sure we respect what he had created."

It is a bit didactic and too obvious, and I think I'll be dropping that add-on. Either the story resonates already as it is, or it doesn't. My hammering won't help.

I love the beauty of oral tradition and how it can wing a story into flight with many feathers. Here's a variation I learned years after that first one: It wasn't by clawing himself out of the ground that Odziohozo created the lake. Instead, the last things Odziohozo couldn't work loose were his legs, but when he finally wrenched them out of the ground, they left behind the deep trench that filled with water.

Since then, I've heard other variations of the Odziohozo story. The one that startled me most was when I was in southern New England and somehow had gotten into conversation with someone about Odziohozo, and they said: Oh yes, Odziohozo who created our lake.

I was immediately offended and defensive. In

fact, it gave me, in a small way, maybe some of the same reaction felt by those offended by an appropriation experience. I felt: Odziohozo is OUR lake creator!

And then I heard the teller's version: that after Odziohozo was up on his two new legs, he went stomping around New England, and everywhere he stomped, he created a lake.

It was such a beautiful rendition. I immediately felt ashamed that I had been so territorial about the story. And the more I thought about it, the more this expanded version endeared the story to me, and opened my eyes to what should have been obvious but never had been to me.

I had always assumed that the various tribes were completely separate and independent. But of course they weren't. They were connected by land and geography, and of course they intermingled and traded and shared knowledge and culture and stories.

What makes Odziohozo so much more of a beautiful story to me is not just that it was a common story, in much the same way as Americans have adopted and internalized European fairy tales and Greek myths, but that this wider version of the story makes it a homecoming story. And all humans love homecoming stories. One of the oldest stories we have in written form is *The Odyssey*, which is a homecoming story.

After wrenching himself free, Odziohozo goes on a journey. And he returns. He decides on permanence in the womb from which he was born.

On some cruises, I hold up my wrist and point to my bracelet. My wife had the latitude and longitude of Odziohozo inscribed on this bracelet as a gift for me.

I love the story of Odziohozo and I have an ever-deepening respect for the rock between Juniper Island and Shelburne Point and what it represents. When my wife and I decided to get married, we decided it would be on our sailboat close to Odziohozo. We chose a beautiful day and were so lucky to have it close with a stunning sunset.

# 8

# I Was Warned About This Kind of Work

After we pass Odziohozo, I turn the boat northwest and aim for the south side of green buoy No. 3, on the southeastern corner of Juniper Island.

Vermont and its skyline of the city of Burlington on the shore and the Green Mountains forming the far horizon now lie a mere mile to our east.

On a sunny and dry day, while the sun is still shining from an eastern angle against the Adirondacks, it seems the mountains to the west are so close and clear that I can count every tree over there about eight to 10 miles away.

When I had the sailing business, I would train my crew not to become fair-weather sailors who do a good enough job for a calm day. "Every time a boat casts off," I would repeat ad nauseam, "you should be prepared for anything. Anything can happen."

So coils had to be neat, lines run fair, knots made cleanly. Always.

An emergency release of a knot, line, or coil can just as easily be necessary in the middle of the Atlantic, in 15-foot waves and a driving rain, as it can be on a calm day on Lake Champlain if someone slips overboard in a moment of the very absentmindedness we are trying to induce on such outings.

As we sail between the Adirondacks and the Green Mountains, there's an opportunity to take you beyond the calm of Lake Champlain and transport you elsewhere.

I tell you that on my voyage, one of my favorite passages was sailing my boat through the opening to the Mediterranean Sea, that gap between Spain and Africa that is known as the Strait of Gibraltar.

I point toward the Adirondacks.

"The distance between that shore" —my index finger pointing straight west while raised to my eye, as if my hand were a sextant and I was taking a reading of the mountains; then I drop my hand and turn 180 degrees, and my arm sweeps across the skyline of the Green Mountains— "and the

Vermont shore, is exactly the distance of the Strait of Gibraltar, the opening to the Mediterranean."

I'm surprised by how this little fact, inserted into a two-hour narrative on Lake Champlain, always elicits surprise and a reaction of "Really?" followed by a series of tick-tock head turns to appreciate the transport from Lake Champlain to somewhere between Morocco and Spain's Andalusian coast.

These are the moments I work for. This "Oh ho!" and sit-up-and-take-notice reaction that I hope to achieve with my stories. It is for this reaction that I practice my storytelling. I hone it. Every single time I deliver my little spiels, I am practicing my timing and choosing different words. I take careful note of reactions and modify my delivery accordingly.

When I was about to take on this work, someone warned me against it. "It will be like driving a bus. Is that the kind of mind-numbing work you want to be doing?"

I was drawn to the work and hoped my desire for it would trump the warning, but I worried about that warning all throughout the first year, looking for hints of boredom and routine in the work. Some might say that I worked so hard on the constant refinement as the antidote to that early warning.

But I think it is simply in my nature. I think I knew that part of the reason I was drawn to the business was that I subconsciously knew it would be a way of exploring my relationship to a being with whom I have been in love ever since arriving in 1978. I knew her stories would be an endless challenge to get right.

And now, after years of doing this work, whenever I find the story becoming routine, or my desire to tell it waning, I ask myself a simple question: "Have you fallen out of love with Lake Champlain?" If yes, get out of the business right away. But again and again, I find the answer to a rote and unimaginative rendition is asking myself a simple question, over and over: Why do I love Lake Champlain so much?

Maybe the way I'm telling the story is stale and I have forgotten why it's important. Maybe it's a lapse in gratitude, a lack of appreciation for how special this place is and what it means to me.

Sometimes, because of time restraints or the general mood of the group, I have to leave out some stories. It isn't easy. They seem to be part of the mandatory repertoire. Not telling them feels like cheating you out of the full profile of the lake.

For instance, I might say: "Some of you are later going to get on your devices and find out that Odziohozo is not called Odziohozo. And you're going to call me a liar again, because what you will see is that the rock is called Rock Dunder. So, just so you know that I know my waters, I'll tell you how that rock got the name Rock Dunder."

And then I explain how "dunder," a variation of damn or thunder or God's wrath, used to be a politer way of swearing, and so the rock's modern name is actually an old swear.

Then I go on to say how, after the first sea battle at Valcour Island between the British and the Americans, during which the Americans were defeated, the remaining American boats retreated overnight. The next morning, the British went hunting for the Americans in the fog. They fired on one ship for quite some time before the fog lifted and someone yelled, "It's just a rock, by dunder."

It wasn't the only rock to which that happened that day. Another rock was dubbed the personal prize of the British commodore after being fired on. Carleton's Prize is a rock between Stave Island and South Hero.

The story always gets a chuckle for the renegade rebels having a laugh at the reigning global superpower of the day.

In my first couple of years as a tour guide, I would tell the Rock Dunder story first to get it out of the way and then leave the guests with the more emotional Odziohozo story to digest while we sailed by.

In later years, I reversed the order and told the Rock Dunder story last. I would wait for a while, giving the homecoming Odziohozo story time to sink in, and then pipe up with something like "There's another story to that rock."

I found myself rushing through the Rock Dunder version, even though I knew it would get that oh-so-desired chuckle.

Why was I struggling with it?

I couldn't come up with a good answer, but I followed my instincts one day and decided not to follow up with the Rock Dunder story. I decided to let Odziohozo own the rock and the story. Why not?

It felt awkward, but in the silence that followed,

I watched people look at Odziohozo and then pull out their devices and snap a photo.

I wondered what they were thinking. We each make up our own meaning to a common story, but only if it's universal enough to touch an evolutionary nerve.

# 9

# *Juniper Island*

As we sail past Odziohozo and head toward Juniper Island, I allow some time for the group to find its own vibe. Often this is when you begin to show interest in each other.

Before we set out, while we were still at the dock, I went around and asked everyone if they lived here or if they were visiting. Now that you have listened to me for a while, and we are out in the lake, you turn to each other and begin to share that you know the city or region where someone else is from. And the conversation cascades into that wonderful American phenomenon called small talk.

Someone inevitably asks about the pine-shrouded chunk of land that sits prominently at the southwestern entrance to Burlington Bay.

Ah, I say, you mean that country over there? That independent republic in the middle of two U.S. states? It is called Juniper Island, and its story leads directly to the story of how New York City became the center of our country's economy and finance.

We think that New York City naturally became that center because... "Well, just because," I say while nodding as I get reciprocating nods from my New York-centric guests. Yes, just because, and after all, it is situated where a river meets the ocean, so it was only natural.

But it wasn't natural at all. In fact, our major city back in the early days was Philadelphia. That was our most important city. That was the U.S. capital in the late 1700s. In comparison, New York City was tiny and had no real significance.

I know, I know, I say. "You ask about Juniper Island, and here I am talking about New York. Please, bear with me. We will end up back at Juniper Island because the story of New York City is connected to the story of Burlington and to Juniper Island."

The story starts in the late 1790s and early 1800s, when this country still hadn't fought its last war against the British. The idea of connecting the Hudson River and Lake Champlain was proposed and rejected a number of times. Some of the problem was that, while Europe had experience with building canals, America had never built something on the scale that was being discussed. The idea of a canal system quickly expanded into that of a canal between the Hudson River and Lake Erie, some 360 miles due west through the wilderness.

Keep in mind that this was before the advent of the steam shovel and before the refinement of TNT and dynamite. The workers would have to use shovels, pickaxes, and the dangerous method of black powder detonation to clear the way through rock. The whole idea was derided as foolish.

At this point, while we are sailing closer to Juniper Island and we can already make out the individual trees on the island and the pebble beach on the eastern side, I beg my audience for patience.

You asked about Juniper Island and we're getting there. But first you have to appreciate the canals that connected Lake Erie, Lake Ontario, and Lake Champlain to the Hudson River, because we are talking about the largest public works project in America at the time. The cost was outrageous, both in dollars and in the lives of the Irish and Italian immigrants who were imported just to work on digging a ditch in the wilderness and forced to live in squalor in company-owned camps, where they had to pay most of their earnings back to the company for supplies. It was a crazy project. It was the kind of frenetic development that would give rise to that fevered entitlement with the euphemistic name of manifest destiny.

It also resulted in the first American wave of explosive economic growth. With the completion of the Erie Canal, an entire barge of goods could now be transported in a matter of six days from Detroit, Michigan, to New York City. A trip that used to take weeks by horse and wagon.

Trade exploded in the Northeast. And it wasn't just the material goods that were being reloaded in New York onto other boats that set sail for ports all over the Americas; all of this had to be financed. And all of this had to be insured.

And it wasn't just goods from the Midwest. The canal to Lake Champlain opened first, and that's what gave Burlington its jump-start into the market of global trade and transformed Burlington from a sleepy little town into the Queen City.

One of my favorite anecdotes of the kind of changes brought about by the canals to Lake Erie and Lake Champlain involves all the secondary business that such changes bring about. Before the canals opened, Philadelphia and Boston had the most jewelers: three times the number of jewelers in New York. But within a decade of the canal opening, that proportion inverted, with New York City becoming the jewelry center of the nascent United States.

And what made New York New York made Burlington Burlington. Immediately upon the opening of the canal connecting Lake Champlain to the rest of the world, Vermont started filling barges with goods like stone, ore, agricultural goods, and lumber.

Lots of lumber. So much lumber that within a couple of decades, Burlington was one of the largest lumber-shipping ports in the Americas. By the mid-1800s, Vermonters had chopped down nearly every single tree that could be milled and shipped.

I turn toward the Green Mountains and I say that today in Vermont, we see a landscape that is mostly forested. But in the mid-1800s, it was almost all fields.

And that's when we became sheep country. And that's why you—and I nod toward a Vermont couple—will come across stone walls in the middle of the woods. They nod back enthusiastically.

And that's when we started to build the woolen mills and textile mills, I say, and point toward an old, three-story brick building with a tall chimney near Burlington's waterfront. Like that one, I say.

It's another "aha" moment, as the New Englanders get all excited and start to talk of the stone walls on their property or their neighbor's. And every New Englander knows the stories of the woolen mills and how they were abandoned following World War II in favor of cheaper labor in the South. And how these once-thriving towns had nothing left but dairy farms. And Vermont became the second poorest state in the union by the 1960s.

I feel like I am a weaver. These stories I am telling, along with the sights we are seeing, weave together into a tapestry of this region's history.

The shipping industry took a significant hit when rail arrived in this region in 1849. But even with the competition of trains, the Erie and

Champlain canals remained viable, and commercial traffic continued to grow to about three million tons per year as recently as the late 1960s.

It wasn't rail that stole the last jobs away from the captains and deckhands. It was the next large public works project in our country: the Interstate Highway System, built in the 1950s and 1960s. By the mid-1990s, tonnage on the canals fell to less than 50,000 per year.

I don't get into all this detail about the canal system while we are out there on the lake, with the Adirondacks in the background, as we are approaching Juniper Island, but for the last few decades, it has been red ink that flows through the canal system. There simply isn't enough traffic to sustain the operation and maintenance of such an expansive infrastructure. But the canals, especially the Erie Canal, are a huge part of the New York's identity, and the residual traffic through them still contributes to the tourist economies of the small villages along the waterways.

In 2004, according to Wikipedia, the New York State Canal Corporation reported a total of 122,034 recreational lockings, along with 8,514 tour boat lockings and 7,369 hire boat lockings.

The cargo had fallen from the three million tons of the 1960s to 12,182.

Not enough to break even by a long shot, but too much in tourism to lose for the small towns that once were bustling ports and now are plagued by chronic store vacancies and only a small fraction of the population they need to sustain themselves.

Someday the canals will close. I am resigned to it. It doesn't just make financial sense to continue the leaking system, but lately there has also been the issue of the lake's health. Invasive species have been entering through the canals. Zebra mussels now clog intake and drainage pipes in the lake. There is talk of the round goby. And the spiny water flea has already made it into the lake. Both compete with native fish for food. They can also spread diseases up the food chain, which can lead to illness in birds.

The lock masters are already taking measures like double flushing a lock before allowing a boat to pass through, but it is an imperfect measure.

Despite my more rational beliefs and support for fiscal responsibility and living an environmentally conscious life, even when it means sacrifices, I know it will be a sad day for me when the locks close.

I will miss the possibility of getting on my boat and sailing off anywhere in the world. I will miss being able to venture out on grand expeditions and then return through a hidden passageway to the relative calm of a great interior body of water.

The ever-so-slightest tinges of claustrophobia will seep up from my depths if I feel like I am closed in by Lake Champlain.

Why do I feel this way? Why is it important to me that I feel I can escape?

I've always known that this is a foundational element in my relationship to Lake Champlain. I've often thought that, without this ability to sneak out of the lake, I might have settled somewhere else. Some Atlantic coastal town. I like Portland, Maine, a lot. In my early thirties, I lived just up the road in Rockland while I was working on a windjammer. Since then, I've been there by VW camper and with my own sailboat during one of my voyages from Lake Champlain to Casco Bay. During my brief stopovers, I've gotten the sense that Portland has a similar vibe to Burlington.

Perhaps the answer to my need to have ocean access is as old as humanity itself. Why did

Odysseus take an additional 10 years to return home from the war on Troy compared to all the others? Because there is something in us that wants to explore the unknown.

That is why we put humans in gigantic firecrackers and send them off into space.

When it comes to sailors, there is an unspoken hierarchy. At the top are the global singlehanders, all following the first known one: Joshua Slocum, who on April 24 of 1895 set off from Boston and sailed solo around the globe just to say that he did it.

Just below that are any sailors who have completed an ocean crossing, and even more respect goes to those who have completed several. And somewhere on the same level of respect, but of a slightly different scale, are the liveaboards. A different scale because some of them never leave the territorial waters of their homelands, yet the commitment to living aboard requires skills, sacrifice, and a certain temperament that landlubbers can't muster.

Below those groups are the weekenders, day sailors, and regatta crews. Some of them might be far more skilled in close-quarters maneuvers than the ocean-going liveaboards who set the sails and never have to touch them for days in a row. In the estimation of some, regatta crew rate at the pinnacle of sailors.

To me, sailing has always been about the romance of the voyage. The chance to get away. The lure of living simply and in harmony with nature, staying on the hook in her moods, and plotting a course through hazards and currents when the conditions are favorable.

To me, sailing has always been about the unknown. The next. The beyond. So to close off the hatch on the southern tip of the lake is saying "end of discussion" and walking away.

There is the northern exit.

Lake Champlain drains out, on its northern end, into the Richelieu River, which flows into the St. Lawrence, which leads to the Atlantic. But that route is long and arduous. The current in the St. Lawrence is strong. There are few ports in case something goes wrong. By going down the Hudson, one can reach the Caribbean single-handedly through coastal cruising and with anchorage in a safe cove every evening. To exit the lake through the gushing St. Lawrence is a thousand miles longer and is equivalent to an ocean passage for which one needs experienced crew.

# 10

# *Ok, for Real Now:*
# *Juniper Island*

I promised to tell you about Juniper Island, and instead I rambled on about the canal and New York City.

Sorry for the digression, but the story of Juniper Island starts with the opening of the Champlain Canal.

I point south and say that when the canal opened down there, boats would head north, and when they saw Juniper Island here, they would take a right and be in Burlington, but at night, well, then they would end up on Juniper Island.

It gets a chuckle, but it's another lie, and I admit it right away. There is no story I can find of a shipwreck on Juniper Island. Before the U.S. government bought Juniper Island from the then landowner and built the lake's first lighthouse station, shipping companies paid private land-owners to keep bonfires going to help captains navigate at night.

Supposedly there was also candlelight on a pole on Juniper Island. The new lighthouse on Juniper Island was modern technology. A Fresnel lens around a wick fueled by whale oil. It required daily cleaning of the lens. Living out on the island with a family required self-sufficiency.

Electricity came along in the 20th century, and the old light was replaced by an automatic light on a steel skeleton tower near the lighthouse.

And here's where things got interesting. In the 1950s, the government decided it was a waste of money to maintain the island just for the auto-mated light, so it offered the island to Vermont.

Vermont declined. When I came to Vermont in the late 1970s, Vermont was the second poorest state in the nation. If the government didn't have money to maintain the island, Vermont certainly didn't, either.

The government turned to New York State. Well, here's the thing: The Adirondack Park, all those mountains we are looking at over there, is a six-million-acre state park. It's the largest gov-ernment-owned park in the lower 48 states. The

Adirondack Park is larger than Yellowstone and the next largest park combined.

New York certainly didn't need another 13 acres, and so it said no.

At the time, one of our state senators was a man by the name of Fred Fayette. I slow down and enunciate his name slowly and clearly because that name will be the punch line. And because I change my delivery, all heads turn toward me as I say what Fred Fayette said to the government: "Wait a minute, I have an idea. Why don't you auction off the island to private ownership?"

"And guess who won that auction?" I ask.

You all smile as we arrive at the punch line.

But here's the best part. Do you know what the Fayette family hat says?

The Republic of Juniper Island.

The U.S. government auctioned it off and neither Vermont nor New York wanted it, so there it is: an independent little nation in the middle of the lake.

The story never fails to get snickers.

And often a cynic quickly asks: So they don't pay any property taxes?

I hate that question. Not because it is the pin in the balloon I just so nicely blew up, but because it reduces everything in the U.S. down to an anti-government sentiment.

My father came from a line of manufacturers and started his own factory in Brooklyn, which he later moved to Vermont. I thought he was the greatest capitalist who ever lived because, while he believed in capitalism as an economic system, he was a strong believer in government and saw government as the parental guide to the selfishness of capitalism. He told me that whenever he met another golfer griping about taxes, he loved delivering the line "Taxes? I hope that someday I owe a million dollars in taxes."

The owners of Juniper Island do pay taxes, I say. I lie through my teeth as I explain that the family, in a goodwill gesture, has negotiated a tax rate with the City of Burlington in much the same way the city negotiates with the University of Vermont and other supposed nonprofits.

I say I was lying through my teeth, but I swear that somewhere, on some long-defunct website, I saw something that gave me that impression.

But here's the thing, I say. It's not about the taxes. The taxes are small potatoes. The real story was about gambling and high-end tourism.

Here is the best part of the Juniper Island story. I have long forgotten where I heard all this:

Island owner Fred Fayette knew a man by the name of Dennis Morrisseau. Dennis, or Denny as he was known, was the founder of Leunig's restaurant. Some may recognize his name and remember Denny's "Westward Ho" program in Burlington, which provided homeless people with a one-way Greyhound ticket out west.

Anyway, Denny and Fred got to talking, and by the end of the first bottle, Denny says to Fred, "You know, if this is a republic, then you can put a casino here."

I remember my feelings back when I first heard the story: I didn't know the lake the way I do now, but even back then I felt that a casino would have been a betrayal of sorts. A selling-out of the lake in a way that tainted Burlington. In a way that catered to the rich rather than the working class.

Fred agrees with Denny, but only in theory. It isn't something he is going to do. And that's why Denny asks for the island after Fred dies. And in my telling, after the second bottle of whiskey, they write up what I call a napkin deal.

Upon Fred's death, when the whole estate

ends up in probate court, guess who's knocking at the judge's door on Monday morning with a napkin in his hand?

You smile again and say his name: Denny.

Denny fervently believed that he deserved to own the island.

In a complicated court case that dragged out to 20 years and was appealed all the way to the Vermont Supreme Court and became the longest case in Vermont history, Denny lost. The island remains in the hands of a group of family heirs.

And that's why today, as we are looking at this island, we see it forested instead of having a hotel, casino, and helipad.

After I'd told that story that way for years, it finally rose to the top of my list for winter research. I couldn't go on lying like that forever.

What I ended up on was a little voyage all its own. A voyage in search of some truth to my story.

I started by contacting the City of Burlington. To my surprise, but even more so to that of the clerk who emailed me back, Juniper Island indeed wasn't in the city's tax jurisdiction. This made the clerk curious, and his surprise became near-incredulity after he contacted the surrounding towns and received the same answer.

So it was true! The island didn't pay taxes! Now I wondered how I would answer that pesky question. The best way to get answers was to contact the family itself.

I remembered that a fellow captain had been asked to take former governor Howard Dean out to Juniper Island so Dean and his party could visit the old lighthouse. They had gotten permission from the current owners of the island.

I invited that captain to breakfast at the Parkway Diner one January morning and I asked him if he could give me a contact for the family. He said he could, and later that day, he sent me a name with a text number.

I texted. I said I wanted to talk to the owners about their feelings about the island. To my delight, I got a message back that day.

"Hi Mathias, very nice to meet you! Absolutely, would be happy to have a conversation with you about Juniper Island. Cheers."

I invited him to breakfast at the Parkway.

I had kept my invitation general. I wasn't going to ask about taxes. I already had that information. What I wanted was verification of the casino story. That is the better story. Maybe this owner knew the story. That would be well worth the eggs, bacon, and coffee.

But I was becoming more and more interested in what it might feel like to be one of the owners of the island. And I was drafting questions in my head, which circled that theme.

What does it feel like to own Juniper Island? Do you have any memories you could share about being on the island? Do you know of any geomythology about the island? Have you camped out and seen the stars?

Meanwhile, I decided that it might be helpful to get other balls rolling. What if the owner got cold feet and declined a get-together? Or if we met and he didn't know anything about the casino? After all, the casino was the brainchild of two owners ago. First old man Fred Fayette, then his son, and then the current group of heirs.

I sent an email to a lawyer who had represented me over a decade ago on some real estate matters. She loved this inquiry. She began her research and roped in another real estate lawyer from a collegial firm.

By Friday afternoon, I had something from him in my inbox. It was a concise historical record of the island compiled from digital copies of newspaper clippings.

As I browsed through the material, my breath was almost taken away when I came upon an image of an article on the front page of the *Vermont Sunday News*, March 3, 1957.

The article was reporting on an interview CBS had aired with State Sen. Frederick J. Fayette. This was just months after he had been the top bidder (at $7,000) for the island during a federal auction in November.

In that article, Fayette is quoted as saying: "I might re-name it 'The kingdom of Juniper,' in which case I naturally would be king of the island. Then, after proclaiming its independence, I would take necessary steps to create ministers with and without portfolio and to arrange exchanges and diplomatic missions."

This quote reminded me of a term we used in journalism when we got quotes like this: pay dirt.

This was all the evidence I needed, from the horse's mouth, that the family really does consider the island to be a republic.

I also love that Fayette had actually researched this idea and had found the official term of "minister without portfolio," which means a member of the executive branch of a government who is appointed to a ministerial position without being assigned to head any specific ministry or department.

I love it. But I might have one thing wrong. It's not the Republic of Juniper Island. Excuse me. It's the Kingdom of Juniper Island.

I looked forward to meeting the owner and asking him if it was true that the family had hats printed with that moniker.

It took a while to hear back from him, but eventually I got an email with apologies for the delay. He said he couldn't meet because he lived in West Palm Beach during the winter. But he answered my questions about the casino in his email.

All lies, he more or less said. "Fred and Dennis were never friends and Fred never promised Dennis the island."

So was Dennis just some random person who tried to claim ownership upon Fred's death?

It was time to find Dennis and get his side of the story. It wasn't easy finding contact information for him. All I could find was a post office box in southern Vermont. I mailed him a letter with my questions. But alas, I never heard back.

While waiting for his response, I went back over the email from one of the island owners. He wrote that when the island was sold by the U.S. government at auction, "the international waters designation remained with it." And that led to many people, inside and outside the Fayette family, speculating about a casino and hotel operation.

My eyes returned to the phrase "international waters designation."

As a sailor, I know that the general rule is that a country can lay claim to the waters up to 12 nautical miles offshore. And I know countries take their international waters very seriously. While crossing the Atlantic, I apparently sailed into Canada's waters, and a huge military plane swooped down low over my boat and hailed me on the radio to ask where I was headed and who was aboard.

While traversing a strait between a Greek island and Turkey, I was approached by Turkish coast guard agents who reprimanded me for not flying a Turkish courtesy flag from my starboard spreader.

Could Juniper Island lie in international waters? It isn't 12 miles offshore. The entire width of the lake is only about seven miles at that point. The island lies two miles off Burlington's Oakledge Park and one mile off Shelburne Point. Maps show the island in Vermont territory inside a dotted state line running down through the middle of the lake.

But maybe, because the lake was bordered by two countries, and it was navigable by international maritime traffic, it had its own designation?

A basic search confirmed that, interestingly enough, there is no formal term of "international waters" in international law. The 12-mile rule is a generally agreed-upon standard, but meanwhile the United Nations Convention on the Law of the Sea, signed in 1982, recognized exclusive economic zones extending up to 200 nautical miles offshore.

I bet that any efforts to create a casino on Juniper Island would quickly send lawyers to their pencil sharpeners and confirm, legally, that the island is within the jurisdiction of the State of Vermont and subject to its development laws.

But taxes, no. The Kingdom of Juniper Island does not pay taxes.

As we round Juniper Island on the west side, the side with steep cliffs, my eyes wander up to the ridge and I am taken back to my late twenties. I was living with the woman I would later marry and with whom I would have a daughter. She encouraged me to buy a 19-foot Lightning. It was a wooden boat. A small, open-cockpit daysailor. One weekend, we sailed out to Juniper Island, and I was so ignorant of how boats worked that I didn't know how the anchor worked, so I hauled the heavy boat onto the small gravel beach.

We had brought along camping gear.

We started up the narrow trail through the shrubbery and poison ivy. I don't remember much about the abandoned lightkeeper's house, which would have been in ruins during that time from a fire in the 1960s. Maybe it was caused by someone just as romantically ignorant as me. An innocent bonfire gone awry. We poked our noses into the old lighthouse. Did we go up? I can't remember.

What I do remember is that we wandered to the northwest corner of the island, where a grove of taller pines had created a soft, needle-covered floor that was the perfect bedding for our tent. We went to sleep, but were woken a while later by music. We crawled out of our sleeping bags and the tent and saw one of the ferries in the distance.

Back in the day, the ferry company hosted live bands and dance events. I felt offended that this sacred space and virginal silence had been invaded by landlubbers with noise that could just as easily be organized in some hall in Burlington. But soon, the boat drifted south and its thumping beat faded into the night.

We were left alone again on the small island under a dome of stars.

I love being outdoors at night. On Juniper Island, it was spectacular. The stars shine so much more brilliantly so far from the city.

We pulled our sleeping bags out of the tent on the soft, pine-needled floor and looked up. The stars were all congregated in a band running through the center of the sky. It was as if all the stars were in a river, caught in a tide, and they are, and it's called the Milky Way.

These days, I live in the house in which I first lived when I moved to Burlington at age 18 and I moved in with my father. He has died since and now I live here again.

It's in an area of Burlington called the Hill Section. When I take my neighborhood walk, I come by an intersection that affords an open view of

Burlington Bay, and in the middle of that view is Juniper Island.

I will often pause at this intersection and look out at the lake and Juniper Island.

If it is evening, I will wait for the Juniper light to flash. It flashes white every four seconds. There is nothing more calming than seeing this flash. I silently count the beats between flashes. It is a heartbeat. Something I can rely on. Something that implies, "All's well."

# 11

# Have You Seen the Lake Monster?

We are on course for Lone Rock Point. North northeast. What about the lake monster? someone will ask. Tell us the story of the lake monster.

I don't know why I am reluctant to talk about Champ. I know I have to. For those who have heard that Lake Champlain has a lake monster, it is the whole purpose of booking a cruise: to hear about the monster. To possibly catch a glimpse of its arched spine as it surfaces.

Maybe I don't want to talk about Champ because I don't want to be a party pooper and admit that I don't believe in our sea monster whose existence has been rumored for hundreds of years. Or maybe it's because the way I believe in Champ is more complicated than can be easily summarized and delivered as a fun story.

I know a captain who tells the story of being a child on a small sailboat with his father in Malletts Bay. It was a dead air day and their boat was becalmed. Suddenly, there was something in the water pushing the boat sideways. After a while, the motion stopped just as quickly as it had started and they were becalmed again. The experience shook my friend to the core. Something is down there. He knows it. He felt it.

Another tour boat captain I hang out with says that when he is asked about Champ, he answers, "I don't drink on the boat."

He says he has practiced delivering that line in a way that always gets a laugh.

When I told him I was struggling with how to talk about Champ, he said I should tell the story the way he once heard me tell it when I came out with him on one of his cruises as a guest captain.

When God created the world, she didn't want to get her hands dirty, so she used glaciers to carve out the lake. She carved so deeply that the Atlantic Ocean rushed in and created a huge inland sea just like the Chesapeake. All manner of sea creatures were swimming around in the Champlain

Sea. Like whales, whose bones have been found and are now Vermont's state fossil. And surely dolphins and perhaps giant squids, and who's to say there weren't animals similar to plesiosaurs among the sea creatures?

Over time, the land rose and closed off the Champlain Sea from the Atlantic. This happened slowly, and the sea creature parents called their children and said, "Let's go! The entrance is closing!" But one child was obsessively playing on its device and said, "Not yet, I'm about to get my high score."

And that's how one of them got stuck in Lake Champlain and has been here ever since.

The part about the inland sea and the land rebounding after the end of the ice age is true. I like my little twist about the child getting left behind. But I never mentioned God creating the world with glaciers instead of her hands. That is purely my friend's version of what he supposedly heard from me. I like it. It's beautiful. So visual.

He's another oral storyteller. It's what we do. We repeat versions of each other's stories. We've been doing it for thousands of years.

We all believe we are telling the story exactly

the way it was handed down to us, but we're not, are we? We're always embellishing. Refining.

When asked whether I have seen Champ, I say this, and this is absolutely true, word for word: I've sailed many bodies of water in the world, and there's a phenomenon I see on Lake Champlain that I have never seen anywhere else. It's a small crest of foam, like from a wave, about six inches high and maybe anywhere from five to 15 feet long, and it moves along at the speed of a sailboat, as if something large is surging just beneath the water's surface. I see it maybe half a dozen times on the lake throughout the summer.

You are not impressed by this report of mine. My guests never are.

Except when it happens. Then I'll stand up and point to a small wave moving along in the middle of the lake.

"See?! Right there!" I swoop my arm around and point out that there are no boats around to leave a wake like that.

Now you react with dumbfounded looks. Everyone stands up and stares and says, "Huh!" And you just keep staring and repeating, "Huh!" Some of you take out your phones and snap a picture.

In his definitive book on Champ, *The Untold Story of Champ: A Social History of America's Loch Ness Monster*, Robert Bartholomew researches every single reported sighting of Champ going all the way back, hundreds of years.

He says Champ wasn't called a monster at first, but instead a sea serpent.

The sea serpent of Lake Champlain became such a national sensation that it came to the attention of P.T. Barnum, who offered a substantial reward for it in 1873, dead or alive.

According to Bartholomew's research, all this attention and publicity and hunting for Champ became known far and wide and generated tourism to the lake. Only then, decades after the first Champ sightings, came the first reported sighting of the Loch Ness Monster. Perhaps Scotland was jealous?

One of the most telling sightings in Bartholomew's book involves a local who said he saw Champ and added, "I went to the house to get my gun, and by the time I got back, it was gone."

That is so reflective of the American love-fear relationship with nature. Our instinct is to conquer. Kill. Own.

It is frightening to have the ability of cognition

and yet not recognize or understand what surrounds us.

Do I believe there is an ancient sea serpent under that wavelet moving along out there a few hundred feet from the port beam?

Maybe the answer has something to do with this: My sister, Nicole Dubilier, is a scientist at the top of her field. She is a director at the Max Planck Institute for Marine Microbiology in Bremen. She travels all over the world to study what lives in the ocean. She has made some stunning discoveries of creatures we did not think could exist. Creatures without mouths or guts or excretion systems, and yet they are fully functioning beings. She leads teams of scientists out on oceanic research vessels, and they study entire animal communities thriving in the dark deep sea without sunlight, which we didn't think was possible not too long ago.

She tells me that we have higher-resolution images of the moon and Mars than of most of Earth's seafloor and that far less than 0.01 percent of the seafloor has ever been directly observed by us, either with our naked eyes or through remotely controlled vehicles. "Which means," she said, "that almost all benthic (deep-sea-living) habitats and communities remain unseen."

That shocked me. It continues to humble me. It makes me mad when I hear we are vacuuming up rare minerals from the ocean floor to make batteries for electric cars when we don't even know what ecosystems we are disrupting by doing that.

The attitude of not-knowing leads to exploration. The attitude of knowing leads to exploitation. I prefer to say I don't know when it comes to Champ.

I felt like I had finally reached the depths of my feelings for Champ with that statement. It was a nice, smug little line that I could deliver on my next cruise.

Until I said it to my sister.

"I disagree," she wrote in a letter that was an elegant defense of science. "This is why scientific knowledge is essential for protection and responsible stewardship: you cannot protect what you do not know." She concluded her many additional points by saying, "Scientific inquiry... strives for deep, integrative understanding rather than the distortion of findings to justify exploitation."

Ouch! She had eviscerated my tidy little answer and classified it among the very attitudes

I railed against: distortion to justify a smug little answer.

While what she had written was true, it left me, once again, at a loss for why I am so reluctant to say I don't believe in Champ. Or, more accurately, why I keep on trying to figure out exactly how I do believe in him, or it, or something.

Maybe this: To me, Champ isn't a question about a creature. It's a question about questioning itself. Why not question?

Instead of banning wonder, I prefer an open mind and inviting possibility.

Why not, when looking out across this immense organ called Lake Champlain, wonder? What is causing that ripple?

Wonder is an invitation to exploration.

Lake Champlain invites.

# 12

# Cliff Jumpers and a Drowning

As we get closer to Rock Point, I'm keeping a sharp eye out. Every boat, every kayak.

"Constant Bearing, Closing Range" is the old rule I teach my deckhands. If an approaching boat always stays proportionally on the same bearing—say at two o'clock to our course of noon—and we keep closing the range between us, then we are on a collision course. These days, there are fancy algorithms on digital devices that calculate the time and location of the impending collision. I have found those helpful when I am crossing the ocean and the other ship is so far away that the bend of the horizon hides it, but on Lake Champlain, it's fun to return to the old ways. Sharp eye estimating bearing and range. Frequently, I will maneuver to give way when in fact I have the right of way. Most boat operators don't know the rules on water. There's nothing to be gained by getting upset about it. There's plenty of lake.

I also look for anything that doesn't look normal. My eye lingers for longer when I see swimmers.

Early one summer, I saw one who wasn't moving in the way you get used to seeing people moving in the water. This one wasn't swimming, nor were they treading water. It was more of a bobbing. They were much farther offshore than anybody normally swims. I hardened the jib and steered the boat that way. I passed close and was able to check in with the person. He was struggling. He floundered at the surface and his words were not coherent. I tossed a life ring right next to him and told him to hang in there while I came around again to get him out.

As I looked over my shoulder, I was stunned to see him push the life ring out of the way and swim a few strokes toward us. Oh right, I remembered from training with an EMT: People struggling for their lives are not logical.

"Man overboard," I announced as we began the procedure for which I had trained my crew at the beginning of the season. My deckhand lowered the mainsail, and I fired up the engine. We came around to our swimmer again, with furled sails, idling motor, and ladder lowered over the gunwale. With both my deckhand and me hauling him up, limb by limb, we got the young man into the deckway of the boat. He lay there, exhausted, only semiconscious. I ran down the list of questions I had been taught to ask. Did he have any medical issues we needed to know about? Was there someone we could call? No, there was no one. He just needed to rest. We covered him in blankets. Even though it was summer, his core body temperature had been dangerously lowered by the 60-plus-degree water.

My deckhand took the helm and headed back to the dock while I tended to the young man. Once I knew he was stable, I finally asked him what had happened. What were you doing in the water so far from land?

At first, his answer came in fractions of sentences.

Swimming.

Over there.

Across.

New York.

I knew he had to conserve his strength, but I couldn't help but ask another question. The burning question. Why?

What came out, in a calm voice, sentence by sentence, in between labored breaths, was a tale of love. They hadn't been together for too long. She had broken up with him. She lived over there. Across the lake. He wanted to do something heroic to prove his love for her. To win her back. So he decided to swim across the lake.

I felt so many emotions simultaneously for this young man. What a fool to set out across the lake if he wasn't a well-skilled swimmer! And yet part of me was deeply moved. I couldn't help it. I am, at my core, every bit the romantic he was. I understood his desire and that it was all the more noble for its apparent foolishness. Isn't that the essence of love? That it is willing to take on any obstacle, in the face of reason, against all rationality, just to prove that love can be unconditional?

I looked out across the uncrossed lake as my deckhand motored us toward the harbor. I didn't know exactly what I felt as I stared out across nine miles of water. But I knew that I should register that feeling and examine it some future winter in my quarters on the hill.

As I remember that event, I know what I might have been feeling.

Something along the lines of the feelings that Alfred Lord Tennyson wanted to awake in us in his poem "Ulysses" when he wrote the lines:

*There lies the port;... / There gloom the dark, broad seas.*

...as he was describing a tired Odysseus contemplating something, once again, heroic.

Odysseus looks at that sea and thinks,

*Some work of noble note, may yet be done...*

To me, there is a direct connection between that poem written in 1833, at the ascendancy of humans' dominance of the seas, and that young man's hope that his heroic act would salve the heart he had wounded. Which brings us to the lake's responsibility for the drowning man.

Let us not just blame the young man as foolish.

Let us recognize that the lake has the power to seduce us with fantasies. We know how the lake spoke to him: I am worthy of your most enduring demonstration of love.

I know because the lake has seduced me.

First in small craft,

then in larger and larger vessels,

then into becoming her guide

her host

her steward.

I looked down at the wet man lying in the deckway of my boat. I tucked the blanket in around his neck.

"It's all good now," I said. And knew I was just saying something. Something that was a lie, but that would hopefully ease the pain in this young man that wasn't going to heal for a long time to come.

I apologized to my guests that the cruise had been interrupted and said I would refund their fares. But I could tell from their reactions that they had gotten to experience something unexpected but worth more than what they thought they had come for.

# 13

# Cliff Jumpers: For Real

With any luck, if it's an average summer day, I get to show you some cliff jumpers, now that we're close to Lone Rock Point.

I never heard of anyone jumping off the cliffs at Rock Point when I was a teenager in Burlington. It's a thing of this new generation. I keep wondering how it became a thing. Why has it become so popular?

The two cents psychologist in my head says it's because danger has become minimized. Kids aren't in tune with the reality of possibly becoming a quadriplegic. Or maybe it's the opposite: Being on their devices so much has made them bored and yearning for the thrill of something real. In any case, it's a thing now.

There are two jumps. One, a minor thrill. The

other downright dangerous. The first is about 12 to 15 feet from the islet rock and the other is from a spot high up on the cliff above the water.

There are almost always jumpers on the rock. It requires a short swim of perhaps 20 or 30 feet, and then a scramble up a steep boulder to a platform.

It takes a bit of maneuvering to get the boat to line up parallel with the rock so that you can watch as the young people psych themselves up and jump off the rock.

In the last few years, I have been seeing young men up the challenge and do backflips into the water. Only once have I ever seen someone dive headfirst. The surprise was breathtaking.

The steeper jump, from the peninsula cliff, is probably around 40 or 45 feet. This jump is always done feet first, arms tight to the side. Though sometimes there is some midair flailing, and I worry about whether they are going to make a clean entry.

Not everyone does. There are rumored injuries. This past summer it was someone who broke both arms. I keep the boat's motor running at idle and run through a mental checklist of the man-overboard retrieval procedure.

Everyone's device is out to capture the jump. When the jumper surfaces, the whole boat explodes in applause and cheers.

I'm always nervous.

I want to be the one shouting: "Don't jump!"

You don't have to.

There is nothing to prove.

Not to others.

Not to yourself.

I am taken back to my sailing voyage through the Mediterranean. We left the boat at a marina near Dubrovnik and rented a car to Mostar. We didn't know about the Mostar Bridge, but found out as soon as we were in the city center and standing on the pedestrian stone arch bridge, which towers about 75 feet above a river and spans between two medieval towers.

It was full of people crowded on one side of the bridge, and we soon found out why. A young man in a bathing suit was making the rounds and asking for donations before jumping.

There was something bizarre and uncomfortable about the situation. We were standing on a gorgeous stone bridge, and I wanted to learn more about this ancient city. But here was this "theater" being performed. An act of daring that was consuming all attention. I couldn't help but feel a bit of sadness or pity for the young man.

The town had been demolished during the recent Bosnian War. Some buildings were still riddled from bombings and artillery fire. This town was trying to claw its way back to economic prosperity, and was this the answer? Having its youth be circus animals?

Another part of me was already pulling out my wallet and fishing out money for his collection bin. After all, I was there. I was a tourist. I was part of the crowd. It was quite possible that this was indeed the most lucrative and stable way to make money for himself and possibly for his family.

The young man was wearing shorts, three-quarter length with ragged cuts, making them look like pirate pants, except he had modified the pockets with zippers to keep his money safe while he dove. He didn't wear a shirt and his youth was on proud display. He kept stuffing the money into his pocket without looking. It didn't matter how much you gave as long as you gave.

Then he climbed up onto the wall, and I was near the edge and I could see over the wall and the river below.

He faked and feinted for a while, riling up the

crowd. Teasing them. Holding out his hat and asking for more, and the crowd gladly gave it.

I was enjoying his little show. As a fellow crowd entertainer, I could see how well he had perfected his timing and moves. It was impressive.

Then he turned toward the river and the crowd got quiet, because this time we believed he really would. And then he did. So quickly and smoothly that it was as if he simply slipped from our view. And there he was, diving like an Olympian, folding first, then straightening, and then there was the river's swallowing splash. There was a silent wait. Silence among a hundred people on the bridge, and then the explosion of cheer as he comes up through the surface, raised fist in the air.

I have always appreciated that while Burlington relies on tourism for a good part of its economic success, it has not become a Provincetown or Key West or Mostar.

The jumpers at Lone Rock Point jump for their own reasons, but not for money.

Another port I visited was the town of Kotor in Montenegro. It is the most intact and preserved walled, medieval town I have ever visited. It was fascinating to have to park outside its walls and enter through an arched entrance that was built hundreds of years ago. We allowed ourselves to get lost in the small town's warren of narrow alleys, and we stopped to examine the fortified entrances and imagined troops repelling an ill-considered attack.

But what gave Kotor its charm was that it was still inhabited today by people in the same apartments and living quarters that were built hundreds of years ago. It hadn't transformed into a mere theater or stage set. It was still itself. Proud, but also poor, and when we looked into the apartments, we could see just a bare bulb dangling from the ceiling over a room with a bunch of kids on mattresses on the floor, and on one of them was a mother nursing the youngest.

I struggled with liking Kotor for its "charm" of being "real" and with seeing that the reality was poverty and a small town that had once been a center of trade during the Venetian era, but today had no internal industry to sustain it.

Except for tourism. Except for gawkers like me who were peering into their shabby apartments and looking away quickly to instead focus on the ancient methods of fortification.

Dubrovnik, up the Adriatic coast by a day's sail and in the neighboring country of Croatia, is an example of what happens when a town becomes no more than a caricature of its former self. Dubrovnik is many times the size of Kotor and, similarly, is an almost perfectly preserved fortified city from the medieval era.

But its massive walls and defensive towers were no match for the modern-day warfare of the Bosnian War in the early 1990s. Dubrovnik was eviscerated by bombings, snipers, and finally by large-scale looting and torching. About 16,000 residents were evacuated by sea.

By the time I visited, about two decades later, Dubrovnik had become a poster child for overtourism. The only shops sold postcards, sunglasses, or linens, and the only other establishments were restaurants.

Every day, cruise boats arrived and disgorged thousands of tourists. They shopped, clicked photographs, and overran the outdoor restaurants, but few of them stopped to read the plaques that described the most recent war and how it drained the city of its permanent residents.

My respect for Kotor and its inhabitants deepened when I learned the town had decided to limit cruise boat traffic. The town had seen what unrestricted tourist traffic does to its neighbor

Dubrovnik, and despite its poverty, it turned away from that soul-numbing flow of cash.

I was keenly aware, whenever I visited a new place in the Mediterranean, that I was a double-edged sword. Income, but also one more reason the place had to perform or somehow appear as something that would tease out more money from my wallet.

And so we have arrived at another conflict within me. Nested inside the others. Like a more inner Russian doll. Lake Champlain is special. I hope it always remains special. A bit less traveled. A bit discoverable. Rather than overrun.

Hoping for that, wanting that, and yet making tourism my business is a conflict.

I can find excuses. One excuse is to say that Burlington is not overrun yet. There is room for more tourism without tourism dominating our way of life. But that is a faulty argument. Because the logical conclusion is not to contribute to tourism before it becomes dominant.

Another excuse goes to a deeper reason that motivates me: I want to get people to appreciate nature. I want to get you to appreciate nature using Lake Champlain as an example, an emotional template. Maybe you'll go home and allow yourselves to feel something new during your next walk along the Charles, or your drive over the Hudson. Maybe I can get you to wonder about what home means to you. And what kind of relationship you want to have with home.

I remember taking a water taxi tour of the Intracoastal Waterway in Fort Lauderdale, near where my father lived at the time. We knew it was touristy but felt like we had to know what it was like if we wanted to be locals who knew what the area had to offer. So we took it. I don't remember much except that most of the tour guide chatter was about which gazillionaire owned which property. I didn't learn a thing about the history of where we were.

And then, one day, it happened. I found my purpose. My raison d'être. Not just a justification for what I do, but a reason. I found out what my tours can mean to some people. It took me by surprise.

I don't remember the weather that day, but I do remember the couple. They presented as just average. Middle-aged. Middle class. Middling interest in any particular story. I remember this averageness of them because later I would be so surprised that, of all the people to come aboard and make such an impression on me, it should be them.

In a lull between my stories, the woman of the couple asked me, "Do you like your job? Do you like this going out on the water every day?"

I laughed. I thought they were joking. "C'mon," I said. "Look at this. I'm the luckiest man in the world!"

The woman remained serious. She thanked me for saying that. She told me that she and her husband both worked in a cinderblock warehouse with fluorescent lighting. They loved going out on boat tours like mine whenever they traveled someplace new. It was their favorite thing to do. On one of their recent trips, they had asked the captain that question, and he smugly answered, "Just another day on the water." They were so angry at the captain. She told me: We didn't tip him.

So maybe I'm doing something more important than I thought. Maybe this job of mine is helping people in more significant ways than I ever recognized.

Whenever I have doubts about my profession, about whether I am selling out Burlington, or whether I'm just in it to make a buck, or any of my questions about tourism in general, I remember that couple.

This tour is their relief.

This outing on the water, which they always seek out, is how they tolerate their lives. They need Lake Champlain. They need water. They need what it does. Absorb.

We have time to watch one more jumper; then I turn the boat around and head south, toward the harbor.

## 14

# *The Sunset:*
# *Forgiveness*
# *and Promise*

The sun is setting. For the last hour, I've been showing you a variation on the outstretched fingers trick. I stretch out my hand toward the horizon. I hold my four fingers folded at 90 degrees so my fingers are horizontally flat against the skyline of the Adirondacks.

"At our latitude, every finger is 15 minutes," I say. "That's how we know how long it is until sunset." All of you do it right away. You position your pinkies on the mountains and measure how many fingers between skyline and sun. About a finger and a half right now. Sunset in just over 20 minutes.

The hand is the oldest tool of navigation. Our first measuring of the stars was with spread fingers, a practice still used by sailors today out there on the oceans. When held up to the constellations, every finger is equal to two degrees of distance between the stars.

So everyone can enjoy the sunset, I slow the boat to a drift and turn it sideways. The conversation ebbs to silence and things whispered in ears.

The sun is warmly orange, and easy to look at. Its bottom arc is already behind the Adirondacks. The mountains are various shades of blue, with the one closest to the shore a darker shade and the ranges farther back in various hues of lighter blue.

Overhead, the sky is beginning to darken on its eastern edges, over the Green Mountains. There are hints of more colors in the air. Yellow and, oddly, a pale green, but also shades of purple.

I can tell that today we will have a spectacular post-sunset sky because there are high cirrus bands of clouds that are already turning pinkish. Soon, after the sun is completely hidden beneath the horizon, it will offer a dazzling light show by turning the long fingers of clouds shades of dark orange and red.

The reason we have the world's most stunning sunsets on Lake Champlain is proportion. I've seen countless sunsets behind the flat horizon of an ocean with no other features than that flat line in the distance. I've seen sunsets in the Rockies. What makes our sunsets so intimate and engaging is the proportion of a single body of water to a range of mountains only an armful of miles away.

The mountains, the setting sun, and the lake all align, and by doing that, they seem to hint at some greater alignment in life that is beyond our comprehension but worthy of our curiosity.

On this particular evening, with just the right clouds refracting the light just so, the sunset completely envelops us. Everything is so beautiful, it makes you wonder if indeed there is some sense to this mad existence here on planet Earth. Visible, possibly, to some others out there in the galaxy.

Sunsets are so powerful because they are a personal messages to each of us. To me, every time, it's a message of forgiveness. It's a message that all will be well.

The day, along with all of its tumult, is absorbed into warmness, softness, and the promise of ease.

The sunset is a forgiveness of the day, and a promise of beauty in the future.

Forgiveness and promise. Two of the most powerful forces for us humans. No wonder I experience something I can authentically call awe every time I see a sunset on Lake Champlain.

Even for me, after years of doing this almost every day in summer, it is the sunset that is the highlight of a voyage out on the lake. A reward, and more significantly, a reward that wasn't necessarily deserved, but was given anyway. Unconditionally. What, if not that, is love? That's what suddenly endears me so deeply to nature in the middle of this sunset: gratitude for the gift of being able to experience deep inner peace. Calm. Love. Awe.

# 15

# *This Way But Not Here*

I fire up the engine to head home. On nights like these, I hate to do this. It is such a stark awakening from whatever Elysian Fields I had lulled you into. I feel like a parent who knows it's time to leave the playground, otherwise dinner will be late and moods will get tangled.

I divert from the disappointment by saying how much I enjoy night sailing. It reduces the experience to elementals. Wind pressure on the boat. Heading. Sharp eye for hazards.

Often someone will comment how surprised they are that they can see just about everything even in the dimming light. Other boats. The city glimmering on the shore. The mountains in stark black.

I aim the boat toward the lighthouse on the northern end of the breakwater. I point out that Burlington Harbor's northern lighthouse is flashing red every two and a half seconds. All the heads turn. I point out that the breakwater's southern lighthouse flashes white every four seconds.

I'm not alone in my love of lighthouses, but I belong to a smaller group that has actually relied on them for navigation during a voyage. Here's what I love about them most: They signal something highly unusual and almost contradictory. They say: This way, but not here.

They are almost always at dangerous entrances to harbors and always situated on rocky peninsulas, islets, or other hazards to navigation. We use them to know which way to get home, but to follow a lighthouse to its source would end in wreck and ruin.

On my wrist with the bracelet with the coordinates of Odziohozo, I wear another bracelet, given to me by my daughter, and on it is a pendant of a lighthouse.

She gifted it to me because of my love for sailboats and the sea, but it has taken on deeper meaning to me because I feel that's what I can be for her as a parent. A general suggestion of direction, but my life can't be her destination.

The two lighthouses on either end of

Burlington's breakwater are both flashing: This way, but not here.

I look over at the eastern sky, which is dark blue by now. On a few days every summer, the full moon rises over the Green Mountains at just about this time. When it does, it is red or pink from the setting sun. It hitches my breath every time.

I'm so lucky I live in a place where I get to experience sunsets like ours.

And now, in the dusk, as we are already inside the breakwater and we are approaching the dock, I'm going to give you a final treat. I love this one.

I hold my extended arm straight out with my finger pointing at Juniper Island. I tell you to look and wait and you'll see the flashing light of the tower on Juniper Island, every four seconds.

Every time, there are gasps, and someone might say, "Oh, look!" and raise their fingers in the direction of the flashing lighthouse.

It closes a loop. You are connected now by this flashing and by stories to this body of water. This lake is now a place you know a little bit. And hopefully, by now, you know this is the way to fall in love with a place, even if your "here" is elsewhere.

# *Acknowledgments*

I am grateful to the generations of storytellers going all the way back to when we told each other stories in caves. I'm honored to be of that vocation.

Thank you to every deckie who ever crewed for me and heard these stories hundreds of times and did all the work while the attention was on me. Thank you, matey.

Thank you to the great editor Rachel Carter, who saw what this book wanted to be and helped it become better at that.

Thank you to my sister, Nicole Dubilier, for investing time and thought into my work and holding me to a higher standard than smugness.

To my Great Love, Kirsten, whom I got to know and married on Lake Champlain while heading this way and here, thank you. I am grateful to be yours.

Dear Reader: Send me your stories, memories, thoughts, anecdotes, about the lake and what Lake Champlain means to you. I'm interested. Mail to: Bartleby & Co., PO Box 4141, Burlington, VT 05406.

www.ingramcontent.com/pod-product-compliance
Lightning Source LLC
Chambersburg PA
CBHW021329060726
47591CB00006B/1941